HEAT WAVES

AND WILDFIRES

TRANSFORMING EARTH'S GEOGRAPHY

Published in 2019 by
KidHaven Publishing, an Imprint of Greenhaven Publishing, LLC
353 3rd Avenue
Suite 255
New York, NY 10010

Designer: Gareth Liddington
Editor: Kirsty Holmes

Photo credits: Front Cover & 1 -Christian Roberts-Olsen, 2 - machnimal, 4 - Anna Nahabed, seeshooteatrepeat, 5 - Suwin, Ernst Prettenthaler, 6 - Tom Wang, 7 - Orlando_Stocker, Ranglen, 8 - Andrei Minsk, Robert Biedermann, 9 - LiliGraphie, 10 - bixstock, Tim_Booth, Saikat Paul, 11 - apple2499, Rich Carey, 12 - rotsukhon lam, 13 - Foodio, 14 - Lukasz Pajor, rsooll, 15 - EMJAY SMITH, lapon pinta, 16 - rocco constantino, Neil Lockhart, 17 - StockPhotosLV, welcomia, 18 - Soloviova Liudmyla, Dark Moon Pictures, 19 - Eddie J. Rodriquez, Guy J. Sagi, 20 - Juliann, hugolacasse, Vaternam, 21 - matsabe, Erin Donalson, 22 - venusvi, Janos Rautonen, Puffin's Pictures, 23 - Kzenon, bonzodog, PlusONE, 24 - S.J. Photography, FCG, Bumble Dee, 25 - Bruno Ismael Silva Alves, Dmitry Kalinovsky, 26 - boreala, Geartooth Productions, 27 - BrittanyNY, NASA Goddard, 28 - Tongra239, 29 - Nils Versemann, VanderWolf Images, 30 - Pi-Lens, hovikphotography, castate. Images are courtesy of Shutterstock.com. With thanks to Getty Images, Thinkstock Photo and iStockphoto.

All facts, statistics, web addresses and URLs in this book were verified as valid and accurate at time of writing. No responsibility for any changes to external websites or references can be accepted by either the author or publisher.

Cataloging-in-Publication Data

Names: Brundle, Joanna.
Title: Heat waves and wildfires / Joanna Brundle.
Description: New York : KidHaven Publishing, 2019. | Series: Transforming Earth's geography | Includes glossary and index.
Identifiers: ISBN 9781534528871 (pbk.) | ISBN 9781534528895 (library bound) | ISBN 9781534528888 (6 pack) | ISBN 9781534528901 (ebook)
Subjects: LCSH: Heat waves (Meteorology)–Juvenile literature. | Wildfires–Juvenile literature. | Natural disasters–Juvenile literature.
Classification: LCC QC981.8.A5 B78 2019 | DDC 363.34'92–dc23

Printed in the United States of America

CPSIA compliance information: Batch #BW19KL: For further information contact Greenhaven Publishing LLC, New York, New York at 1-844-317-7404.

Please visit our website, www.greenhavenpublishing.com. For a free color catalog of all our high-quality books, call toll free 1-844-317-7404 or fax 1-844-317-7405.

HEAT WAVES AND WILDFIRES

CONTENTS

Words that look like **this** can be found in the glossary on page 31.

WHAT IS A HEAT WAVE?

Do you enjoy being able to play outside in the summer sun? It's great fun, but what happens if the temperature rises too high? Sunshine smiles can turn into heat wave horror.

Playing in water fountains is a great way to cool off on a hot day.

Humidity is the amount of moisture in the air.

A heat wave is a long period of unusually hot weather. Often, humidity is high, too.

Heat waves can overheat our bodies and cause health problems for babies, young children, and elderly people. Extreme heat waves are dangerous for everyone and can be deadly. They are classed as **natural disasters** and can cause damage to transportation systems, power supplies, and **ecosystems**.

Heat waves in the United States cause more deaths than all other natural disasters, such as hurricanes and tornadoes, combined.

This road in Australia has melted during an extreme heat wave.

4

DEFINING A HEAT WAVE

The World Meteorological Organization says that a heat wave happens when the highest temperature is higher than the highest average temperature for that day and place, by 9°F (5°C) or more. This has to happen for five or more days in a row.

TEMPERATURE GRAPH FOR ANYTOWN

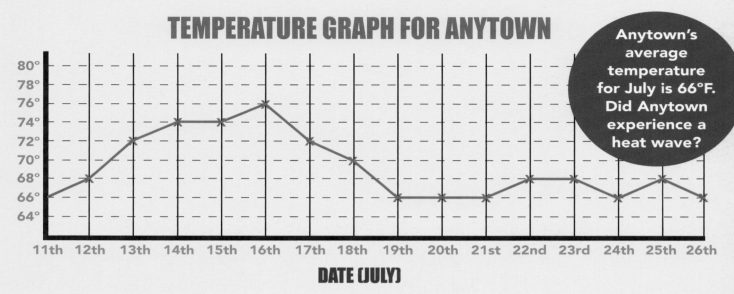

Anytown's average temperature for July is 66°F. Did Anytown experience a heat wave?

DATE (JULY)

The World Meteorological Organization is made up of leading weather scientists, called meteorologists, who study and predict weather patterns.

Temperatures that might be considered a heat wave in some places would be normal in others. The average July temperature in London, UK, for example, is just 66°F. In Death Valley, USA – one of the hottest places on Earth – the average temperature in July is almost 108°F.

Death Valley, California, USA

5

WHAT CAUSES HEAT WAVES?

Air pressure across the world affects wind and weather patterns. Both high and low pressure systems form and move around the globe, producing very different weather. High-pressure systems usually bring clear skies that allow heat from the sun to pass through, heating Earth's surface. Slow-moving high-pressure systems force air downwards, preventing warm air near the ground from rising. The sinking air acts like a cap, trapping warm air underneath.

SLOW-MOVING HIGH-PRESSURE SYSTEM

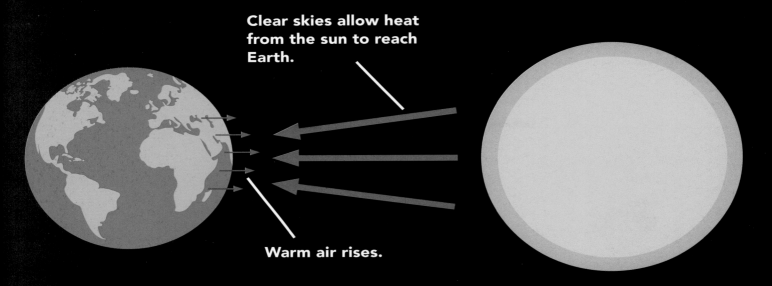

Clear skies allow heat from the sun to reach Earth.

Warm air rises.

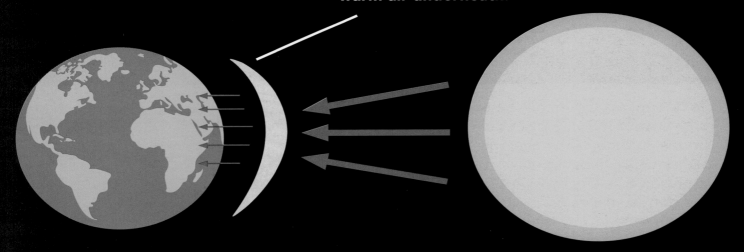

High pressure forces air downwards, trapping warm air underneath.

CLIMATE CHANGE

Climate change – also called global warming – is gradually heating up our planet. Most scientists believe that the burning of **fossil fuels**, like coal and oil, is partly to blame. As they burn, fossil fuels release carbon dioxide and methane, known as greenhouse gases.

Greenhouse gases form an invisible layer around Earth and trap heat from the sun. Scientists predict that in the future these greenhouse gases will help create heat waves that last longer and have higher temperatures.

Emissions from cars and power stations that burn fossil fuels contain greenhouse gases.

Some scientists think that by 2100, almost half the world's population could be in danger from extreme heat waves.

WHERE AND WHEN?

Heat waves happen all over the world, in both the Northern and Southern Hemispheres. The USA and Australia both experience heat waves, as do countries in Europe such as Spain, Portugal, France, and the UK. Certain parts of Asia, including China and India, also have heat waves.

NORTHERN HEMISPHERE

UK

PORTUGAL

USA

SPAIN

FRANCE

CHINA

INDIA

AUSTRALIA

SOUTHERN HEMISPHERE

In 2010, a deadly heat wave in Russia killed tens of thousands of people and covered nearly 400,000 square miles of land.

Heat waves are most common during the summer months. Whereas summer months in the Northern Hemisphere are June, July, August, and September, in the Southern Hemisphere, the summer months are December, January, February, and March.

Heat waves usually develop slowly and can be predicted by meteorologists, giving people time to prepare.

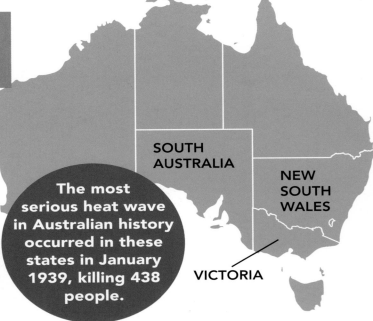

SOUTH AUSTRALIA

NEW SOUTH WALES

The most serious heat wave in Australian history occurred in these states in January 1939, killing 438 people.

VICTORIA

Heat waves can be a time to enjoy the beach, but they can also be deadly.

THE JET STREAM

The jet stream consists of fast-moving ribbons of air, approximately 7.5 miles (12 km) above the surface of Earth. The jet stream affects how weather systems form and how areas of high and low pressure move around the globe. The changing position of the jet stream can bring unusually warm air and higher-than-normal temperatures to a region. In 2003, the jet stream contributed to a heat wave that affected much of Western Europe, causing thousands of deaths.

The jet stream is positioned 5 to 10 miles above the surface of the Earth and can reach speeds of over 200 miles per hour.

1,000 TO 3,000 MILES LONG

1 TO 3 MILES WIDE

THE EFFECTS OF HEAT WAVES

Our normal core body temperature is 98.6°F (37°C). If it rises by only two degrees for a few hours, we can suffer from heat exhaustion, with headaches, cramps, and sickness. If it rises above 104°F (40°C), it can cause deadly **heatstroke**.

Some people are much more likely to be affected by heat waves than others. People at risk include those who work or live outside without proper shelter from the sun and those who cannot afford air conditioning.

This man is cooling off in a public fountain during a heat wave in Calcutta, India, in 2015.

These outdoor workmen in India are likely to be affected by heat exhaustion or heatstroke.

Heat waves can affect food production by damaging crops and livestock. Wildlife and pets also suffer. If the surface of the sea rises 2 to 4°F (1-2°C) above the average summer temperatures, it can cause serious damage to coral reefs, causing them to turn white and die. This is called coral bleaching.

Bleached coral loses its bright colors and may eventually die.

Extreme heat also damages roads, bridges, and other structures. Power supplies are often affected due to the huge demand for air conditioning. Hospitals and health centers may be overcrowded due to health problems caused or made worse by the heat.

During a heat wave that affected Australia in 2018, a 6-mile (9.5 km) stretch of highway in the state of Victoria melted in the extreme heat.

In some parts of Australia, the koala is now a threatened species, due partly to climate change.

SURVIVING A HEAT WAVE

Try to avoid being in direct sunlight. If you do go out, always wear high SPF sunscreen, a hat, and light-colored clothing that covers your skin.

Never leave children or pets alone in parked cars, even for a few minutes.

Check up on elderly or sick relatives and friends.

Take cool baths or showers to lower your body temperature.

Use a fan to keep yourself and your pets cool.

It is best to eat cold,
light meals during a heat wave.

Avoid **strenuous** and outdoor activities, especially during the hottest part of the day from 11 a.m. until 3 p.m.

Drink plenty of water and if you do have to go out, make sure you have water with you.

Eat light, cold meals. Try to avoid high-protein foods, like meat, that raise your body temperature.

Turn off lights and other equipment that give off heat.

Hot air rises, so keep to the ground floor or basement of your home, especially for sleeping. Try taking a cold water bottle to bed – put it in the freezer for a few hours before you go to sleep. Hang a wet sheet in front of an open window to cool the room down.

HEAT WAVE IN EUROPE, 2003

In July and August 2003, a heat wave in Europe led to the hottest summer in around 500 years. Many European countries recorded their highest ever temperatures, including the UK, where a temperature of 101.3°F (38.5°C) was recorded in Kent, England, during the heat wave on the 10th of August. Temperatures remained at record high levels, even at night. At least 30,000 people died across Europe. Many farm animals died, including cows, pigs, and chickens. Crops also died, including the French grape harvest. Wheat production in France was reduced by 20%.

The London Eye had to be closed during the 2003 heat wave due to extremely high temperatures in the viewing pods.

Damage to wheat and other crops led to higher food prices.

The heat wave was caused by a nonmoving high-pressure system over Western Europe that trapped warm air beneath it. The clear skies and lack of rain that high pressure brings turned the heat up to record highs. Most scientists agree that global warming was also to blame.

In some countries, **reservoirs** and rivers used for public water supplies and for **hydroelectric power** stations either dried up or ran very low. The high temperatures melted **glaciers** in the Alps, causing **avalanches** and flooding in Switzerland, where a record temperature of 106.7°F (41.5°C) was recorded.

The Alps, Switzerland

WHAT IS A WILDFIRE?

A wildfire is a large, destructive fire that burns in an area of **vegetation** such as woodland, bushes, or grasses. Wildfires burn fiercely and in an uncontrolled way. Although they usually occur in **wilderness** or rural areas, they can spread to places where people live and work, burning homes and businesses.

Wildfires often begin unnoticed but quickly increase in size and spread over large areas. Wildfires usually happen in places with a warm, dry climate, often following a heat wave that has dried out vegetation.

Wildfires are also called forest, grass, peat, or bushfires, depending on the type of vegetation.

A forest wildfire in Nevada, USA, threatens the nearby city.

Ground fires are slow-burning and burn **organic matter** in the soil. Fires that burn on the surface of the ground are known as surface fires. They spread quickly, burning twigs, fallen branches, and dry leaves. Crown fires burn from treetop to treetop. They spread rapidly and burn fiercely with intense heat. Winds may blow balls of fire, known as firebrands, away from crown fires, starting new blazes. Wildfires can travel at an amazing 10 to 12 miles (16 to 20 km) per hour, destroying everything in their path.

Firefighters tackle a surface fire.

Due to the long, hot, and dry summers, wildfires are very common in the southern areas of Australia, where they are known as bushfires.

Crown fires jump from treetop to treetop.

WHAT CAUSES WILDFIRES?

Heat waves, **droughts**, and climate change all increase the chance of wildfires happening. Wildfires can occur naturally. They may be caused by intense heat from the sun or by lightning. **Lava** and flows of very hot ash, rocks, and gases, called pyroclastic flows, from erupting volcanoes can also start wildfires.

Lightning is a natural cause of wildfires.

More than four out of five wildfires are caused by humans. Areas of wilderness are popular with campers, but a campfire left alone can quickly start a wildfire. Cigarettes or matches that have been carelessly thrown away while still lit can also be to blame.

Campfires that are left unattended are a common cause of wildfires.

In places where humans live close to areas of vegetation such as forests, the threat of wildfires is great, especially during dry, hot summers.

Sparks from bonfires, fireworks, equipment such as metal-working tools, power lines, and car accidents can all accidentally start a wildfire. Sometimes wildfires start when large areas of vegetation are cleared to make way for farmland. What starts as controlled burning can quickly get out of hand. It is hard to believe, but sometimes wildfires are begun deliberately by people.

The act of setting fire to something deliberately to cause damage is called arson and is a serious crime.

Trees falling across power lines can start a wildfire.

HOW DO WILDFIRES BURN?

Fire is a **chemical reaction** that gives off light and heat. In order to burn, a fire needs fuel, **oxygen**, and heat. Firefighters call this combination the fire triangle. Without any one of the three, a fire will not burn. Some factors make a fire burn more fiercely.

Have you ever noticed that a gust of wind makes a bonfire burn more fiercely?

Winds provide a fresh supply of oxygen. They can direct a wildfire or cause it to change direction to areas with a fresh supply of fuel. Winds can also tilt the flames forward. This preheats and dries out vegetation in the path of the fire, helping it to spread quickly.

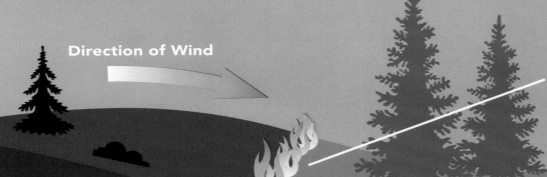

Direction of Wind

Preheated vegetation ahead of the flames catches fire easily and causes rapid spread.

Burnt Vegetation

Wind supplies fresh oxygen and directs the fire.

Dry tree bark can carry fire up to the treetops, allowing the fire to spread rapidly.

Wildfires usually move faster uphill than downhill. The steeper the slope, the faster they burn. High temperatures and sunshine dry out vegetation – the fuel for a wildfire. Places with this pattern of weather are much more likely to experience wildfires than cold, damp areas. High humidity reduces the chance of a wildfire because there is more moisture in the vegetation, which makes it harder for the fuel to catch on fire. How fast a wildfire spreads depends on the type of fuel. Lush, green vegetation slows a fire down, whereas dead, dry vegetation speeds it up.

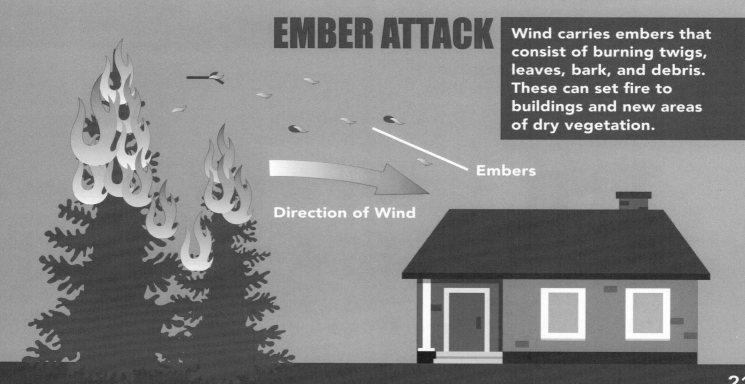

EMBER ATTACK

Wind carries embers that consist of burning twigs, leaves, bark, and debris. These can set fire to buildings and new areas of dry vegetation.

Embers

Direction of Wind

THE EFFECTS OF WILDFIRES

Ash and smoke cause air **pollution**. This can cause breathing problems and other damage to human health.

People may be killed or injured. In 2017, dozens of people were killed and injured in Spain and Portugal. Wildfires were fanned by winds from a hurricane in the Atlantic Ocean.

A forest is a complete ecosystem. Wildfires upset the balance of this ecosystem, damaging vegetation and wildlife including birds, rabbits, and squirrels.

Water used by firefighters can cause soil erosion.

Homes, property, and businesses may be destroyed. People may lose their jobs and income. People may be forced to evacuate their homes to avoid danger.

Wildfires can cause serious damage to soil. They can raise soil temperatures to over 1,650°F (900°C) and damage organic matter in the soil.

Wildfires are very expensive. As well as causing damage to property, they are also expensive to fight. Costs include firefighters' salaries, chemicals, and equipment such as fire engines.

The water supply to an area may be damaged by ash and debris. Wildfires may also affect normal drainage of water into the soil, and this can lead to flooding.

Wildfires have a long-term effect on the appearance of an area. They damage tourism and the jobs that it supports. But some jobs can be created by a wildfire, for example repairing and rebuilding property.

Wildfires release a great deal of carbon dioxide, a greenhouse gas, into the atmosphere. Trees absorb carbon dioxide and other harmful gases and release oxygen into the atmosphere, but during a wildfire trees are destroyed.

FIGHTING WILDFIRES

FIREBREAKS

Firefighters try to deprive a wildfire of its fuel, so that it goes out by itself. They use bulldozers and tree cutters to clear an area of vegetation ahead of a fire. This creates a firebreak. When the fire reaches the firebreak, it runs out of fuel.

Firefighters use a hand tool called a pulaski – a cross between an ax and a hoe – to help them dig firebreaks.

Pulaski

A firebreak has been made in this forest in France in case a wildfire should break out.

AIR TANKERS

Air tankers are aircrafts fitted with large tanks containing thousands of gallons of water, foam, or **fire-retardant chemicals**. The aircrafts empty their tanks ahead of the wildfire to dampen vegetation and slow down the spread of the flames.

Air tanker

HELICOPTERS AND FIRE ENGINES

Helicopters move firefighters quickly to where they are needed. Bambi buckets are buckets suspended underneath helicopters that are used to dip water from nearby rivers and lakes to drop ahead of the fire. Fire engines can carry over 800 gallons (3,000 L) of water and hundreds of yards of hose to help firefighters attack a fire at close quarters.

Firefighters wear clothing made of a fire-resistant material called Nomex and carry a tent-like fire shelter to protect them if they are trapped by flames.

DRONES

Drones are unmanned aircraft. They give firefighters a bird's-eye view of a wildfire and help them figure out where a fire may spread. Drones carry wind sensors and special cameras that can see through thick smoke.

Drones can fly in conditions that would be dangerous for air tankers and helicopters, for example in thick smoke or at night.

This drone carries cameras.

CALIFORNIA, USA, 2017

California is an area of the United States where wildfires are common. The wildfire season of 2017, however, was the most destructive on record. More than 9,000 wildfires broke out. In October, blazes swept through areas of northern California. The counties of Napa and Sonoma were very badly affected. In December, a series of wildfires broke out across southern areas.

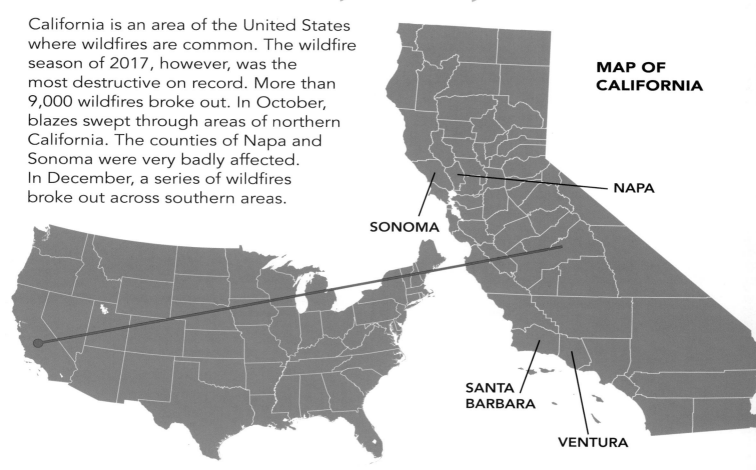

MAP OF CALIFORNIA

NAPA

SONOMA

SANTA BARBARA

VENTURA

Damage Caused by the Thomas Fire

The Thomas Fire burned over 270,000 acres in Ventura and Santa Barbara counties and is the largest ever recorded in California.

High amounts of rain had fallen early in the year, causing vegetation to grow rapidly. Very dry months, with little or no rain and high temperatures, followed. This dried out the vegetation, producing plenty of fuel for wildfires. In southern California, strong autumn winds, called the Santa Ana winds, are well known for fanning the flames of wildfires. In 2017, these winds were unusually powerful and long-lasting, whipping up fires that burned out of control. From space, **satellites** above Earth recorded clear images of plumes of smoke from the wildfires in California.

The Santa Ana winds are known as devil winds because of their effect on wildfires.

This wildfire burns fiercely in Ventura.

This satellite image shows smoke from the wildfires in California. The red spots show actively burning areas.

AUSTRALIA, 2009

Southeastern Australia suffered one of the worst heat waves in its history from the 27th of January to the 8th of February, 2009. Much of Victoria, South Australia, and northern and eastern Tasmania were affected by intense heat. Record high daytime and overnight temperatures were reached. In Hopetoun, Victoria, a temperature of 119.8°F (48.8°C) was recorded – a Victoria state record. More than 370 people died from the heat wave in Victoria. The heat wave was caused by a slow-moving, high-pressure system over the Tasman Sea. Global warming was also to blame.

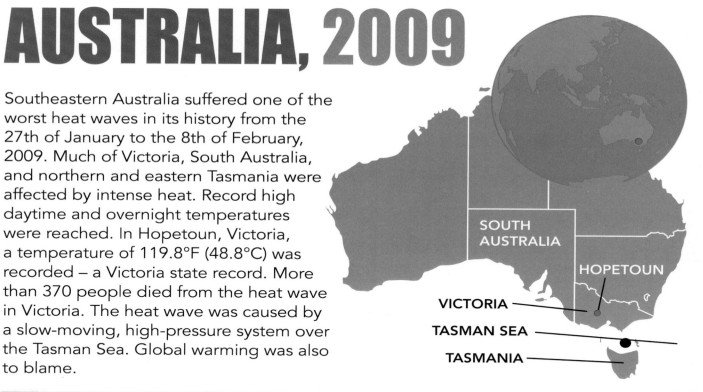

SOUTH AUSTRALIA

HOPETOUN

VICTORIA

TASMAN SEA

TASMANIA

The very high temperatures, low humidity, and strong winds were perfect conditions for wildfires (called bushfires in Australia) to break out. A series of around 400 bushfires began on Saturday, February 7, which became known as Black Saturday. Lightning strikes, damaged power lines, and deliberate acts of arson started the fires. They were not fully contained until the 14th of March. At the height of the blaze, flames jumped 110 yards (100 m) into the air. They were fanned by gusts of wind up to 68 miles (110 km) per hour.

This is a fire danger rating display board in Melbourne, Victoria.

This bushfire has reached the road, which has acted as a firebreak to help contain the blaze.

FASCINATING WILDFIRE FACTS

WILDLIFE WINNERS

Sequoia trees and other conifers rely on wildfires to release seeds from their cones and to clear the soil and tree canopy for new growth. Smoke, heat, and burned wood also help some plants to grow.

New seedlings are appearing in this forest just two months after a wildfire.

FIRE DEVILS

Fire devils form when rising heat and turbulent winds combine to form a whirling funnel of flames, like a mini burning tornado. The funnel sucks in burning material and scatters burning debris over a large area, creating more fires.

Burned soil and vegetation repel rainwater, stopping it from draining away. Wildfires also destroy the organic material in soil that helps rainwater drain away. This can cause mudslides and flooding.

GLOSSARY

air pressure	the downward pushing force exerted by the weight of the atmosphere that surrounds the Earth
avalanches	large masses of ice and snow that move quickly down a mountain
chemical reaction	a process in which one or more substances are changed into other substances
droughts	long periods of very low rainfall, leading to a lack of water
ecosystems	everything, both living and nonliving, that exists in a particular environment
evacuate	move away from an area to escape danger
fire-retardant chemicals	substances that slow down or stop the spread of fire
fossil fuels	fuels, such as coal, oil and gas, that formed millions of years ago from the remains of animals and plants
glaciers	slow-moving masses of thick ice
heatstroke	a serious condition caused by prolonged exposure to high temperatures, resulting in exhaustion, seizures, and even death
hydroelectric power	electricity that is generated using the power of flowing water
lava	molten rock that has erupted from a volcano
natural disasters	violent, natural events that kill or injure people and damage property and the environment
organic matter	living and dead organisms such as plants and animals together with the nutrients from decaying organisms
oxygen	a colorless gas found in the air that is needed by all plants and animals to survive
pollution	the act of introducing to the environment something that is poisonous or dangerous
reservoirs	man-made lakes used to store water
satellites	machines in space that orbit planets, take photographs, and collect and transmit information
soil erosion	the wearing away of soil, due to the action of wind and water
strenuous	something that requires a lot of energy or effort
tourism	the action of visiting new places for pleasure and the industry that supports this action
vegetation	the plant life of an area, including trees, flowers, grasses, vegetables and vines
wilderness	a wild and natural area where very few people live

INDEX